INTRODUCING

Hinduism

by Malcolm Pitt

HEAD OF DEPARTMENT OF INDIAN STUDIES
HARTFORD SEMINARY FOUNDATION

Friendship Press   •   New York

This book is one of a series of Popular Introductions to Living Religions, which includes the following titles:

Introducing Islam, by J. Christy Wilson

Introducing Hinduism, by Malcolm Pitt

Introducing Buddhism, by Kenneth Scott Latourette
(In preparation)

First Printing September 1955
Second Printing November 1956

Hinduism
Christianity and other religions - Hinduism

Library of Congress Catalog Card Number: 54-10130

Copyright, 1955, by Friendship Press
PRINTED IN THE UNITED STATES OF AMERICA

Contents

An ancient Hindu center in a country district of central India. The temples contain shrines both to Siva and the "descents" of Vishnu.

Introduction

There is no more sobering exercise than the attempt to expound, interpret, and evaluate in limited compass that which is the most intimate, the most valued possession of another people. Particularly is it difficult for a non-Hindu to bring about a real understanding of what Hinduism is. The popular clichés will no longer do. The movements of the moment in Hinduism make relatively invalid an approach from the purely historical point of view. A primarily scriptural emphasis, where none but sectarian canons exist, is equally unreal.

The Western urge for analysis and rational criticism can seem only marginal to a Hindu steeped in his evaluation of the authority of aesthetic intuition. The sources of authority, resting so largely outside the written word and the historic "fact," necessitate guidance in a major shift of emphasis. It is hoped that within these pages a Hindu will recognize his own faith and that the Christian reader will seek further acquaintance following this brief introduction to the Hindu.

Hinduism presents an association of religions, a laboratory of religion, paradoxical, multi-faced; common characteristics, however, dominate its history and evolution. This pamphlet will seek to give an understanding of these characteristics as they bear upon the living organisms of Hinduism today. It will, therefore, be uncomfortably oversimplified to the scholar, superficial to the philosopher, and unsatisfactory to many others. Differences between static and dynamic Hinduism must be left unindicated, and care will be taken not to label every practice engaged in by Hindus as Hinduism.

The real point of reference will be the understanding of the setting in which the Christian movement is seeking to express itself and to communicate the word of God to contemporary man in India.

1

I. The Hindu Mosaic

Hinduism baffles definition. In the broadest terms, it is the religion of the Hindus, approximately three hundred million of them. There will emerge certain characteristics of Hinduism in the subsequent pages, but even these characteristics cannot be defined. Without individual founder, without an officially accepted canon of authoritative writings (except in sectarian groups), the religion has no essential, well-defined patterns. D. S. Sarma writes:

> It is difficult to answer the question—What is Hinduism?—in a way which will do justice to all its varied beliefs and practices . . . Hinduism . . . is more a League of Religions than a single Religion with a definite creed. In its hospitable mansion there is room for all types of souls from the highest to the lowest, and, as one grows in virtue, love, and insight, one can pass from apartment to apartment and never feel that the atmosphere is stuffy or hot.[1]

Neither Hinduism nor any of the numerous "Hinduisms," known variously as Vedism, Brahmanism, and the rest, has ever known, wished, or been able to organize itself into a regulated hierarchy with a supreme head; it has persisted in

---

[1] *What is Hinduism?*, by D. S. Sarma, p. 10. Madras, G. S. Press. 1939.

a "systematized anarchy" and therefrom has drawn its strength.

The strength of Hinduism (as, from another point of view, its weakness) lies, therefore, in an intellectual framework into which there may fit a freedom and tolerance of belief and practice that allows the modern Hindu to claim for Hinduism a universality that may even include, if one is uncritical enough, all the religions of the world. To him there is seemingly little conflict between the presuppositions of his framework and the simple characteristics of any organized religion within or without the Hindu fold.

As Hinduism is the religion of the Hindus, let us begin with the Hindu himself. A generation ago it would have been possible to define the Hindu as one who accepted, broadly and theoretically, the authority of the *Vedas*, and was born in caste. No definition is now more than locally possible. One of the great political parties has recently defined the Hindu as one who recognizes India as his motherland and his holy land. This definition would include in the Hindu family the Sikh (who would rather "include himself out"), the Buddhist, and the Jain. One modern writer has claimed that no exact labeling is possible, but that if a man considered to be a Hindu does not reject this label, and if he shares to any degree any one of the ideas or practices associated with the term "Hindu," the label is not incorrect for him.

Here, then, we present some Hindus.

First, meet Sundaram. He speaks Tamil; his home is in South India. Sundaram is a worshiper of Siva. This he proudly advertises by the imposition of the ash of ascetic renunciation in three horizontal lines on his arms, his chest, and his forehead.

In the fulfillment of a dream of long ago, Sundaram is in Chidambaram, site of a famous Siva temple. He is standing before a porch of fifty-six delicately carved pillars that lead to an exquisite shrine dedicated to Siva as the Lord of the Dance. He has made the journey from his home village because of the influence of a wandering minstrel *yogi*, who sang of the grace of Siva and taught the value of a pilgrimage

3

to the place where a royal devotee once had a vision of the Lord. In his vision, the worshiper had seen Siva, attended by Parvati, his consort, dancing on the seashore, sounding a drum.

Sundaram has many times seen crude representations of this cosmic event and has come to know that there is more significance to the worship of this image than was evident in the religious practice of his village. There he worshiped Siva in the songs of the great devotees, leaving his little offerings upon the lingam, a phallic representation of his deity, seeking to keep the gaze of his heart fixed on Siva.

He understands only vaguely that this image he is now seeing is considered one of the great monuments of Hindu

Siva as Nataraja, copper, South India, probably dating from late eighteenth century

artistic genius; to him it is much more significantly the magnet of his devotion, and for the mere sight of this place and figure he has sacrificed much. It might even be that merely to be in the presence of this Siva could insure for him certain material benefits and spiritual progress.

The figure that has drawn Sundaram to Chidambaram is one of the best known and most lasting examples of the Hindu genius for semantic representation. The elaborate symbols used are the documents of religious education for a people not accustomed to the greater abstraction of the written word. This figure, known as Nataraja, the Lord of the Dance, represents the essential philosophy of devotion to Siva, written in bronze, in stone, or in wood.

Hindu sculpture has been something of a closed book to the usual Western observer, and that which has not seemed to be closed to his understanding has outraged his artistic tradition, inherited so largely from the Greek. The Hindu sculptor and painter has attempted in his artistic endeavor to depict the nature of Reality and the destiny of man. In order to accomplish his purpose, the artist has not hesitated to combine a penetrating understanding of nature, of anatomy, and of the realistic with the most striking departure from and transformation of the same; for art in India, ancient India at least, always has a religious purpose, often conveyed to the public through myth and its illustration.

Nataraja has four arms and a third eye. He wears the Crescent Moon and the Ganges River as ornaments to grace his hair. The cobra, symbol of immortality, is his companion in the dance. For each divine function a hand bearing its symbol is necessary—the drum of the "word" of creation in the upper right hand, the flame of destruction and purification in the upper left. The lower right reassures with the "fear not" gesture of concern for and preservation of the world, while the lower left, in the "elephant-trunk" gesture, points out the source of grace, the raised left foot. The entire figure is poised on a dwarf, the ego, which must be crushed if the Lord is to dance. In the center of a ring of fire that stirs all to life is the serene visage of the One who

5

is actionless in the midst of intense activity, unchanging in the midst of constant flow.

Perhaps Sundaram is aware of the fullness of the meaning of Nataraja. More likely, he is remembering the songs that have come down to his people through the lyric devotion of those who have given themselves to Siva and the myths of his appearances—the songs of Appar of Madurai; of the wandering minstrel, Manikka Vasagar; of Tayumanavar, the devoted mystic.

Sundaram has already spent the day with his happiness. There is still tomorrow—or perhaps he will never leave. But before he turns away, he breathes a little prayer that his devotion may be accepted, and that Siva will generously condescend to dance in the real Chidambaram, his own heart.

In a village of North India, Ram Das sits wedged tightly between his friends as he waits calmly for the last installment of the drama of the deeds of Rama. The Rama Lila festival is almost at an end, and the autumn night will finish much less tranquilly than it has begun. In the scene of the fall of Ravana, the enemy of Rama and the abductor of his wife Sita, all, even Ram Das, will participate. Action will no longer be limited to the formal platform of the drama; the whole village will become the stage. The monkey armies will be discovered, underneath the masks, the paint, and the imposed upright monkey tails, to be familiar village figures. Torches will be applied to the effigies of Ravana and his evil companions, and there will be great rejoicing.

The hero story of the *Ramayana* is of undetermined age and is of the greatest importance as the communication of the ethical and devotional concerns of two great poetic geniuses. The epic narration has had two major literary vehicles.

The first of these, reputed to be by Valmiki, is written in Sanskrit, and has served the purpose of depicting the good life, as interpreted by Hindus, under a personal ceiling. It

6

may be that India's sons and daughters do not read the books of law and duty, but they all know the virtues of Rama and the womanly duties of Sita. In this dramatic epic, Good conquers Evil. The reign of the Good is known as the rule of Rama-Ramrajya—a term broadened by Mahatma Gandhi to be the practical equivalent in Hindu terms of the kingdom of God.

The second rendering of the story of Rama, known as *The Holy Lake of the Deeds of Rama,* is the work of the Hindi poet, Tulsi Das (1532-1623), and is one of the first of the great religious documents of India to discard the classical "perfect" language in favor of the more intimate spoken tongue of the Indian people. For this reason, it is available to Hindi-speaking Indians and, through translation, to those who use other languages. The significance of this recension lies in its devotional purpose.

According to these epics and to the usually accepted view of history, Rama is an *avatara*—"descent"—of Vishnu, the one who preserves the world, guards it from evil, and sends his helpers in time of need. This is the Hindu view of "descent," or incarnation, and is expounded most fully in the greatest of all Hindu books, the *Bhagavad-Gita,* as the common picture of the personal manifestation of Reality, or God, who embodies himself "whenever there is a decline of righteousness and a rise of wrongdoing." Rama is chosen of the Gods to be Vishnu incarnate to defeat Evil as personified in Ravana. Sita, destined to be Rama's wife, is in truth Lakshmi, the consort of Vishnu.

"Descent" in Hinduism is not unique to any single person, but in one sense all are candidates for incarnation. This presents a difficulty to the Christian, for the Hindu is ready to accept the Christian incarnation but unwilling to deny the *avataras* of his own history or those of the present. I have in my possession a poster, found even on railway platforms in India before the assassination of Mahatma Gandhi, that depicts the Buddha in faint outline in the remote background; in bolder color in the middle ground is a picture of the crucifixion of Jesus; in full color in the foreground sits Mahatma

Gandhi, as the incarnation sent to meet the needs of India in the twentieth century.

The story of Rama is that of a dutiful son of a righteous king who has made an unfortunate vow in a moment of weakness: he has promised his junior wife that a younger half-brother of Rama shall reign at the father's death. In performance of his father's vow, Rama accepts banishment and takes with him his ever-virtuous wife, Sita, and a younger brother, Lakshmana. While they are wandering through the jungle, Sita is abducted by trickery and spirited off to Lanka (Ceylon) by the wicked and powerful (yet pious!) ruler, Ravana. The helpers of Ravana are the rakshasas, an order of monsters whose physical characteristics are as distorted as their moral sense. Rama's helpers are the monkey tribes, the chief of whom is Hanuman, who becomes the type of devotee of Rama and Sita. After many vicissitudes, Evil is put down, devotion has secured felicity for the protagonists of Good, and the world is well again.

As he watches the climax of the drama, Ram Das is very much concerned that his wife shall fully appreciate the devotion of Sita to her husband, even when he subjects her to trial after her return from abduction. He also shares with his wife to a degree the joy of Rama and Sita in each other. Above all, he would emulate Hanuman and enshrine the happy pair in his thoughts, singing of them as he works. Just now, he joins lustily with the village audience in singing

> I bow to Rama, the charming,
> beautiful husband of Sita, the righteous,
> To Rama, pleasing as the moonlight,
> To Rama the gracious,
> The Supreme Spirit,
> The Lord of all,
>   We bow.

"That excellent glory of the life-giving god, the Sun—may we attain—may he stimulate our devotions."

With many others, all chanting this same prayer, Narayana

8

stands breast-deep in the water of the Ganges, facing the sun as it rises over Banaras. His hands are folded at his breast, and his head is bowed. This morning his devotions have peculiar significance and are caught up in a tremendous relief from tensions that have complicated his life for some time. His aged father has been desperately ill, and the one wish of the whole family has been that death should come to him by Mother Ganges, so that his ashes may be committed to her breast and his salvation insured. The journey was very difficult to arrange and in accomplishment arduous. For an indefinite period now, Narayana will be away from home. But for the time being, he is content. His duty as the eldest son has been performed, in that his father's dying wish has received effective fulfillment at his hands. And here he will be able to take his allotted part in the prayers, rites, and ceremonies used when death has made the expected visitation.

Established now in a rest house built for just such as he, Narayana is fully ready to complete the assignment of filial duty. In the meantime, he is able to satisfy himself concerning a number of things. He does not completely share his father's trust in the effectiveness of the pilgrimage to Banaras nor in the power of Mother Ganges to grant the final blessing. As much of the day as he can spare from his father's side will be spent in the courtyards of the temples, as he tries to find out how the teachers and the priests will defend themselves when he asks certain questions about which no one has yet been able to satisfy him.

Narayana himself would have preferred to make his pilgrimage to the *ashrama* of a renowned teacher, for he is more interested in discussion of religious questions than in seeking out places made holy as special dwellings of the gods and by significant mythological events.

But concerning his father he is very happy. Just a bit down the river he can see the place where his father's body will be committed to the flames. Already in his imagination he has gone through the acts that it will be his function as a son to perform in the last rites. He will be able to assure his widowed mother that all is well with her husband's soul.

9

Just a few miles away, in the same gray dawn, Professor Sen is preparing a very important lecture for his students in philosophy at the Banaras Hindu University. There is in his mind a great fear that the young rebels in his classes will, in their revolt against some of the social and religious practices of the masses, forget that there is something more to Hinduism than these practices would seem to indicate. He has noticed of late a disquieting tendency to question the very foundation of the most important things he has to say. The spirit of the ancient Aryan culture stands endangered by revolutionary new attitudes toward life and the winds of doctrine that have been blowing over India from the outside world.

Professor Sen has thought it wise to drop, for the time being, the organized plan of the series of lectures in his syllabus. Their subject matter seems to be regarded as irrelevant to the throbbing life of an awakened India by his restive students. To him this is a desperate situation that must be met. He must convince these young potential leaders of India that he agrees with them that the deadwood of the centuries must be cleared away and a new outlook on life brought to bear upon modern problems. But he must make them see that in order to do this, it is not necessary to throw away anything but the lifeless husk of dead custom; then they must retrieve the spirit of the ageless seers of India in the most dynamic eras of her history.

In some way he will have to show that the social, economic, and political aspects of India's life that have usually been associated with the Hindu religion are not an essential part of her spiritual heritage or search, but represent the confining shell that must be broken if the spirit is again to be free. He must also show them that the genius of the creative periods of Hindu history has been the assimilation of new things from within and from other cultures, without the loss of distinctive character; and that the same achievement today means the synthesis of the spirit of India's past and the thorough understanding of the world of the twentieth century, including light from the other religions of the world.

10

As the sun begins to climb the eastern sky, Dr. Sen realizes that in just three hours he has this very responsible task to perform, so he begins to write carefully: "Gentlemen, ———"

In the city of New Delhi stands the Lakshminarain Temple. This is an amazing symbol of the mind of modern India in evaluating her religious past and charting her future.

True to the Hindu genius for symbol in form, this temple, nevertheless, differs from the classic Hindu temples of the past, which are usually dedicated to some one deity enshrined in the dark inner "wombhouse" of the structure. Traditionally, this form of structure is suggestive of the cosmic significance of the object of worship (an image, a symbol), and the worship center is placed to remind the worshiper that the true object of worship is to be found in the inner dark recesses of the heart.

The Lakshminarain Temple is many temples in one: it is constructed with the intent that Sundaram may find there his shrine to Siva; Ram Das may see his Rama and Sita and the beloved Hanuman; Narayana may discuss to his heart's content and listen to the recitation and exposition of scripture; and Professor Sen may meet there the minds of Sankara, of Ramanuja and of Madhva, and of the other pillars of Hindu philosophy. It includes in a single area the different and seemingly irreconcilable points of view of Hindu thought and practice.

And it seeks to be more comprehensive than the label "Hinduism" would indicate, for within *arya dharma* the builders of this temple believe they can include the paths to reality called Christian, Jewish, and Islamic—for do not all ways lead to the One, and are not the differences merely the accidents of history and culture?

II. The Framework

Just as the domes of the Lakshminarain Temple tie together the various aspects of Hinduism, there are certain characteristic dogmatic emphases that unite religious thought and practices into a federal union. This two-forked way of life originated from the content and the use of the earliest religious literature of India, known as the *Vedas*. The function and the content of these *Vedas* will be discussed in the next chapter, but it will suffice here to say that, in terms of content, certain fundamental questions of Reality, the world, and man's relation to these entities have given rise to speculations that result in the various philosophic emphases of Hinduism, ultimately concerned with man's salvation. The characteristic Hindu answer to these questions constitutes the fundamental intellectual framework in which the whole system is set.

On the other hand, the use made of these *Vedas* for ritualistic and even magical purposes has resulted in the ascendency of a group of persons who know them meticulously and who alone are recognized as competent to perform the detailed and involved traditional practices of sacrifice and ritual that have developed through the centuries. This, in turn, has given rise to the peculiar type of social organization that is characteristic of Hindu society, or at least has been characteristic up to the present moment. We will first consider this social organization as that aspect of the framework within which the variety of Hinduism operates.

The legitimate pursuits and life purposes of the Hindu have been traditionally four: *kama, artha, dharma,* and *moksha.*

Kama is the enjoyment and release of the physical energies and urges common to all men.

Artha is the pursuit of business and certain social and economic ends for one's support in the ordinary affairs of the world, group-controlled according to the stipulations of caste and the joint family. These two pursuits, although not necessarily considered religious, have religious implications that are caught up in the other two pursuits of the Hindu with which we will be concerned.

The third purpose of the Hindu is the performance of his duty, *dharma.* This is the only word that the Hindu can use for "religion," but it means that a person takes his place in the order of things by fitting into a predetermined pattern into which he has been born.

Caste is essential to the historical idea of *dharma.* It is exceedingly difficult to write of caste at this fluid juncture in the social history of India. Many of the traditionally valid statements that might be made need constant modification to meet the realities of the moment.

The formidable list of human rights that appears in the third part of the Indian Constitution would seem to say that something very drastic has happened to the concept of caste and its corollaries, the doctrines of transmigration and *karma.* We shall later try to characterize the newer movements in Indian society, but as one thinks historically or looks at many aspects of Hindu society today, one is forced to conclude that a consideration of caste is necessary, since it is the essential social framework that produces, either by revival or reaction, some of the tensions one finds in contemporary India.

The origins of caste are complex, and there have been a variety of theories to explain them. The pious point to a verse in the *Rig-Veda* that attributes the division of society to a divine plan. But in reality caste has been a social and

13

economic phenomenon, with religion playing an important part in its survival and interpretation. It has been the means of integrating into a society more fluid than usually supposed widely divergent groups, leaving them a large degree of autonomy and internal freedom within a social hierarchy demanding strict conformity to laws about marriage, economic function, diet, etc.

Even in the earlier social history of India, as reflected in the oldest writings, we see a remarkable ability to take the discordant beliefs and customs of a variety of racial and tribal groups and weld them together into a loose federation with elasticity enough to comprehend most of the indigenous peoples of India, but with the rigid guarantee of Aryan supremacy at all times, and among the Aryans, that of the Brahman.

This method of integration has loosely been termed the "racial" theory of caste origin—a sort of hands-off, laissez-faire policy to solve the problems of social difference, each group developing with a minimum of interference from others. This is the theory. It was inevitable, however, that such an arrangement could not long endure (or ever exist, indeed) in so ideal a form, human nature being what it is. Fluidity was threatened when village economy demanded fixed occupations for its stability and endurance. Inertia, stagnation, and lifelessness thrived on the social discrimination and exploitation to which caste lent itself with such abandon.

The major division is between the "twice-born" Aryan conquerors and the original inhabitants they conquered. Inevitably there would be a wide chasm between these two groups, socially and functionally. Because of the elaboration of ritual in the all-powerful sacrifices, the Brahmans, the priests and teachers, attained and retained the position of greatest power and prestige. The Kshatriyas, warriors, were next in importance. Other Aryans, usually traders, artisans, and agriculturalists, formed the third major division, the Vaisyas. The Sudras, the conquered people, were the servers. There was a fifth caste, whose occupations rendered them ritually unclean, known variously as exterior castes, untouchables, or, in Gandhi's word, Harijans, the children of God. The Constitution of the Republic of India makes the practice of untouchability a penal offense.

The law codes of Hinduism lay down the ways of *dharma*: the conduct of the individual in his every social relationship, morality in the state, and the obligation to observe usage and traditions. Caste rules control occupation and the boundaries of social intermingling, delimit the matrimonial hunting ground, and concern themselves with food taboos and group discipline. One acts in this world as it is established that his segment of society is supposed to act.

Inevitably corollary to *dharma* are the doctrines of transmigration and *karma*. These are considered by the Hindu to be axiomatic. In spite of the intense variation of thought within Hindu patterns, there is no variation in this. The progress of the human soul, from the time that it appears as an individual entity until it is absorbed into the Absolute again, is a process of education and moral judgment. It is through the continued cycle of redeath and rebirth that the destiny of the individual soul is determined. In the course of this evolution the principle of retribution, the doctrine of *karma* is inexorably effective. "That which one sows, that he shall also reap."

The status of the present embodiment of the soul—spiritual, and even economic and social—is the mean result of the performance of *dharma* in unremembered lives. Because of the unremembered aspects of misdeeds of the past which bring suffering in the present, the doctrine of *karma* comes sometimes dangerously close to a necessary, fatalistic acceptance of one's own lot, as well as the lot of one's neighbor.

It may be well to point out here that in the older understanding of Hindu orthodoxy, caste was the instrument of the moral law in the administration of divine justice. Punishment could be meted out by the fact of social and economic good or ill. If one performed his own duty well, he ascended the social scale—if ill, he fell.

A statement found twice in the *Bhagavad-Gita* and quoted

15

frequently in recent times, particularly by Gandhi, is that it is better to botch one's own job than to perform perfectly that which belongs by natural right to another. "One's own duty" meant, traditionally, his caste *dharma*. Modern writers, however, are considering the performance of one's own duty to mean that one makes the best use, in his spiritual development, of the endowments he has been given. No mention of caste is made, nor is caste even essential to the accomplishment of his goal.

The weight of this responsibility makes it necessary for the Hindu to find freedom. His doctrines of release or salvation are all, expressed negatively, release from suffering the consequences of misdeeds—the inevitable result of being born.

This brings us to the fourth and most significant pursuit of the Hindu—*moksha,* release from the consequences of action and salvation from the necessity of birth and death—release into Reality.

Characteristic of Hindu thought is that this release is possible through certain preparatory disciplines. These disciplines are summed up under the term *yoga.* This term as now heard frequently in the West, is usually associated with a supposed strange tendency of the Indian to make of himself a human pretzel, with breathing exercises and with strange psychic powers. These are of minor importance. *Yoga* is, at once, any one of a number of *yogas* involving moral and contemplative exercises, a dualistic philosophy, and, in general, disciplines preparatory to the supreme experience of realized salvation. These disciplines take, in general, three directions: (1) the discipline, or the way to release, by means of action; (2) the discipline, or way of release, through devotion to a personal deity; (3) and the discipline, or way of release, through knowledge.

To modern Hinduism, the last mentioned way is the supreme one and in this book will be thought of as the metaphysical framework into which one may rationally incorporate the varying practices of the Hindu. This framework, derived largely from the *Upanishads,* is known as the Vedanta, the goal or end of the *Vedas*. It is the "perennial philosophy" referred to constantly in the West.

Without complicating this attempt at explanation by including historical data as to origin and development (see the Chronological Chart, p. 27), we shall state as simply as possible the fundamental and almost universally accepted Hindu theory of the universe. There is one Real Being, supreme above all others, an impersonal absolute, called Brahman. Apart from Brahman, there is no existence, or at least no important existence. As I am conscious of myself, which must to me be real, I am led to the conclusion that my existence is identical with Brahman. This is not an intellectual conclusion, but an intuitive realization that there is nothing else that matters. I am, therefore, not an individual; I cease to use the usual terminology of limitation ("I," "my") and recognize only one existence with many manifestations. At this point I should like to insert parenthetically a reminder of the acute case of academic discomfort this pamphlet has afforded its author. The generalizations so glibly made here all need qualification. In fact, there is no statement about Hinduism that cannot properly be, in some context, denied. The reader will recognize this difficulty and will be sympathetic—he will know, for instance, that the qualifications of the *Vedanta* of Sankara by Ramanuja and Madhava are very important indeed. He will realize that systems other than the *Vedanta* have made telling contributions to Hindu thought: for instance, the dualism of Sankhya, the logic of Nyaya, the physical, moral, mental, and contemplative disciplines of Patanjalis *Yoga*, as well as the systems of the Buddhists and the Jains. All, however, to the same end: namely, the realization of the religious goal of the release of the human soul into its ultimate destiny, however conceived. The emphasis is always on the supreme importance of the soul of man and the disciplines that lead to man's awareness of this fact. We return to the statement already begun above.

Brahman (not to be confused with Brahman, the caste) has been described in the *Taittiriya Upanishad* as "that from

17

which words turn away, not having comprehended with the mind." Brahman is silence. No words can define It; no human idea can possibly probe Its essence, no philosophy can define Its meaning. It is being (*sat*), consciousness (*cit*), and bliss (*ananda*). It is beyond all that constitutes either death or life. It is beyond all concept of knower or the known. It is beyond all interpretation that can be described as pleasant or unpleasant in our finite life. It is inexhaustible. It cannot be held to any limitations whatever. In this sense It is the Absolute, without relation to the world, unsubjected to action or its results. Thus the ultimate aspect of Brahman is unknowable in essence, but It is the real "I." The equation "I am Brahman" is the essence of the teaching of this philosophy.

A second aspect of Brahman is called Saguna-Brahman— Brahman with attributes, with descriptions, with relationships. It is this Brahman, which we may now call "He," who creates, preserves, and permeates the world, and controls its dissolution after its cyclic evolution has been completed. The Christian naturally inquires as to what the purpose of this creation is, existing as it does only as a figment of the imagination, or at least with very little other than relative importance. The answer is never quite clear. A modern Hindu has said:

> As the life of the individual, the growth of society, the trend of human history, and the evolution of life in this world should be regarded as only the different aspects of the one spiritual purpose running through all creation, *viz*, the whole universe returning to God who is its home, it is the duty of every man to utilize his natural endowments and his position in society for the cultivation of spiritual values and, thus, further the divine purpose.[1]

The purpose, then, would seem to be the possibility of final realization by all individual souls of their essential unity. A question may be asked as to why it is necessary to go

---

[1] *What Is Hinduism?*, by D. S. Sarma, p. 131. Madras, G. S. Press, 1939.

through the processes of creation in order that this, already an established fact, may come to realization by individuals who have little real existence. The usual answer is that the purpose supplies no need of Brahman for creation—it is the *lila,* or "sport," of Brahman.

> . . . the self-expansive urge of delight, the outflow of creative joy, the spirit of playful self-expression. Law is the mechanism through which creative joy expresses itself in infinitely diverse forms. So Saguna-Brahman is, indeed, the supreme artist of the world. The world of endless variations is a spontaneous out-pouring of the fullness of his joy.[2]

This Saguna-Brahman we may well term "God" in Hinduism, Isvara. It is as Isvara that most of India knows God— Isvara with his functions, his relationship with the world, and the possibilities of his operation through any channels whatever to relate himself to human beings.

The intuitive recognition of identity with Brahman is contrary to experience; I must, therefore, discipline myself in such a way that that which suggests itself as real, apart from Brahman, must be put in its proper place. This gives rise to the Western criticism of the Hindu as impractical, as other-worldly, as pessimistic concerning the destiny of this world. To the realization of this end, the ancient Indian seeker has removed himself from society, has sought the lonely place, and has discovered the Absolute within himself. The realization of Brahman to the Indian thinker, both in the past and in the present, represents the height of religious attainment.

As corollary to the theory of Brahman, the concept of the world, of the individualization of the life of man and of everyday experiences, must somehow or other be explained. This explanation has traditionally been made by speaking of this world as being at most only relatively real, and in extreme statement, as pure deceit.

Because of the difficulty of basing one's action on this

---

[2] "The Concept of Brahman in Hindu Philosophy," by Haridas Chaudhuri, in *Philosophy East and West,* p. 50, April, 1954.

type of thinking, the Hindu has spoken to ordinary men of the way in which Brahman may be conceived by our more concrete minds. This is where the Hindu doctrine of God, God as the appearance of the Absolute, the Absolute describable as a personal being who has had relationship with the world, comes closest to the heart of the people.

We now become involved in the processes of history, and in time sequence, or chronology.

Chronology is of comparatively little importance to the Hindu. It is no accident that the major great documents of Hinduism are not strictly speaking historical documents, as other great classics are. Even in the mythical stories in the biographies of the devotional saints of Hinduism, legend and fact are so intermingled that it is an almost impossible task for the historian of today, either Indian or Western, to disentangle event from fiction.

It is this writer's conviction that a true understanding of the essence of Hinduism is not primarily the historian's job. It is interesting to note that in small essays about the size of this pamphlet Westerners would be very likely to take up the chronological development of Hinduism through its major documents and documentary periods, whereas the Indian would think of his total history as all one piece in relation to its major outlooks on life. The historian of religion can see the beginning, the development, and the flowering of certain aspects of Hinduism chronologically expressed. But as a religion not fundamentally grounded in history, and with the view of history as relatively unimportant, this development is interesting rather than essential.

An attempt will be made from now on to show something of the chronological relationship of ideas as expressed in authoritative writings. The accompanying Chronological Chart on page 27 will perhaps be of service to the reader in tracing the history of some of these ideas.

Hindu systems of reality in relation to the world and time vary according to sectarian groups. To the Sivaite, the functions of creation, preservation, and destruction, as well as that of the dispensing of grace, are centered in the eternal

Siva himself. To the Vaishnava, Brahman assumes attributes in a triad of personalities performing the functions of creation, preservation, and destruction. The major difference lies in the "descents" of Vishnu the Preserver in certain classical forms to meet world crises and in modern personalities who answer this definition.

Because of the relative unreality of God himself in the theistic sense, the realization that all concepts of God are human and all creatures are Brahman, it seems to be only natural that the Hindu can tolerate the worship of any form of life or any form of any kind as a manifestation of Reality. This is the framework that allows the most advanced Indian philosopher to feel that the most primitive animist, in living up to his best light, is *on the path* to the realization of Reality. It is not necessary that the one who approaches an image as the object of worship know that this is the case in order to have it fit this pattern.

It will be evident now that not only the aspects of Hindu practice suggested by the little stories in the previous chapter, but many more and varied forms of religious practice may be considered truly Hindu in this sense. The pieces of the puzzle of Hinduism fit together within this framework, although each piece may be violently different in color from all the rest.

Gopal Chitra Kuteer

Bathers at Hardwar, a principal center of Hindu pilgrimage

21

III. Religious Authority in Hinduism

From the foregoing, it will readily be seen that ultimate authority in Hinduism rests in persons; not persons who have founded the religion or who have more than indirectly been responsible for prophetic missions, but persons who in themselves have "intuited" Reality. It is the systematized experience of seers and sages that constitutes the body of philosophy. The reverence given in India to the teacher, the *sannyasi*, to the holy man, the *sadhu*, is the recognition of this authority.

For transmission of this type of authority, persons of known spiritual achievement are sought out as they were in ancient times, though today the organization of centers of such teaching and discipline is less informal than in another age. This fact is the secret of the power of such men as Sri Ramana Maharshi, of Sri Aurobindo Ghose, of Mahatma Gandhi, and, to a less extent, many others.

The center from which the influence of such men radiates is the *ashrama*. What makes an *ashrama* what it is, is a person. The picture of a group apart, sitting about in earnest discussion, is as close as we can get to a realization of the way in which the *Upanishads* were produced. These are the documents preserved in great number from the days of the greatest creativity in the thought life of Hinduism. Several (up to the number of ten to thirteen) are considered of authoritative importance and are the basis of modern philosophy, as they were of the classical systems. They are not systematically organized philosophies but are certainly of supreme importance in the presentation of the major concepts that have given rise to the systems. The important thing here to be recognized, however, is the part played by persons in these discussions, for men and their achievements in self-discipline and the impartation of disciplinary means to similar achievement are the purposes of the preservation of the documents.

The transition from the personal to scriptural authority is an inevitable one, and one easy to understand. It is as writings embodying the experience of the adept and recalling his method of discipline to this end that they are authoritative. There are Hindu writings that antedate this major conception, as we shall see in a moment. In days of lean spiritual growth, more and more dependence is placed on the written word, with a consequent decline in the supreme emphasis on a spiritual destiny.

The religion of the *Vedas* was a type of polytheistic nature worship, where the forces of nature were personified as beings who had some control over man. There was in this day no evidence of caste nor discrimination against any segment of society except the Dasyus, who were the conquered people. There is no essential pessimism as to the destiny of the world and of material life. What concerned Vedic man was to live within the order of life so as to please the gods and emerge prosperous and happy. The elaboration of the rules for sacrifice is found in a group of documents known as *Brahmanas*, the *Leviticus* of the Hindu scriptures.

The record of the beginnings of Hinduism is to be found in the literature known as the *Veda*, the body of knowledge. This literature is divided into natural categories of interest and subject-matter. The earliest known religious documents are the collections of psalms (*samhitas*) and charms (*mantras*). Of these, the *Rig-Veda* has been considered by all odds the most important, although the more homely *Atharva-Veda*, concerned as it is with the everyday problems of everyday people, is almost equally valued by the social historian.

The deities who are praised and from whom the goods of life are sought (many years of life, hero sons, cattle and wealth, health) are personifications of the aspects of nature in the realm of the sky (Dyaus Pitr, the sky; Varuna, heaven; Surya, Savitr and others, the sun; Ushas, the dawn, etc.); the atmosphere (Indra, thunder, rain, and war; Rudra, storm; Vayu, the wind, etc.); and the earth (Prithivi Matr, Mother Earth; Agni, fire; Soma, the plant whose juice makes a brew from which Indra, the hero of the days of creation, derives strength for amazing feats.) There is in these hymns a deep appreciation of nature, a genuine poetic quality.

There are also some elements that have great bearing on later Hinduism. Of particular importance is the account of the establishment of cosmic order. Were space available, it would be interesting to recount the myth of the great hero of the gods, Indra, who through his heroic exploits and with the very efficient help of the intoxicating god-drink (Soma), was able to release the sources that make for the welfare and prosperity of both gods and men. He assigned to the various gods their functions in maintaining order, and he relegated the forces of destruction to a proper place below the earth from which they do not come out except to plague man who does not pay proper attention to the gods. The realm of life, light, heat, moisture, and all the benefits of men he separated for man's use. The function of man was, therefore, to perform his appointed task, an idea that is developed by the law books of a later date into the complex functional aspect of caste. When one does perform his function, the purposes of the gods and of the cosmic order are served.

The major function of Vedic man was his recognition of the interdependence of himself and the gods. The gods lived by sacrifice—man's welfare is also determined by sacrifice to the gods. In the midst of this as the general outlook of Vedic man, there are raised some fundamental questions concerning the universe and human destiny.

In the body of literature known as the *Brahmanas*, we find the meticulous explanations of the sacrifice, the ritual that

24

A priest who presides over the conventional small shrine in
which the typical Hindu performs his *puja* (worship sacrifice)
alone

accompanies it and with which the words of the Vedic
psalms are recited. Ritual becomes an end in itself, endlessly
elaborate, bringing with it great personal power to the individual and necessarily creating a specialized group of people
who alone are able to use the materials of sacrifice.

Many of these sacrifices have passed into oblivion, but in

orthodox circles there is still a residue of Vedic practice in ritual and sacrament. A safe prediction would be that, in the not-too-distant future, this artificial aspect of Hinduism shall have passed into oblivion.

It would be an easy trek to pass from the meticulous laws of sacrifice to the development of the social order as outlined in the codes of Hindu law. This has already been indicated in the previous discussion of caste; here we must mention it again because of its significant place in Hindu evolution.

> The Indian caste system, as generally understood, is a system of relationship between stable groups which are largely interdependent, both economically and ritually, and which are arranged in a rigid and accepted order of ranking that is expressed in almost every phase of their interrelations.[1]

There is little need here to emphasize the fact that, although in origin caste may have been a necessary division of labor and a means of amalgamating into Hindu society people who through many centuries were brought under its sway, the time came when the institution became stagnant and lent itself to a love of power, acting as a social strait-jacket. One is constrained to point out, however, that in its ideal, caste was supposed to create a self-sufficient village unit in which exchange of services was on a practical basis. It must also be pointed out that through the twin institutions of the joint family system and caste Hinduism has dealt with the major problems of social security as we view them in the West—unemployment insurance, vocational guidance, care of the aged, and other allied difficulties. It is little wonder that as India realizes that caste has served its purpose and must evolve into something more appropriate to the mobility of the twentieth century and a money economy, she is looking over the world for some organization of society that eliminates the problem of social discriminations and conserves the social good no longer to be had in caste.

---

[1] "Caste and Territory in Malabar," by Eric J. Miller, in *American Anthropologist,* p. 410, June, 1954. Used by permission.

BRIEF CHRONOLOGICAL OUTLINE OF
HINDU LITERATURE, PERSONS, AND RELIGIOUS DEVELOPMENT

Dates Unknown

Concurrent Historical Events and Persons

Vedic Period, Punjab

Mantra (hymn) Period

The worship of the personified forces of nature by hymns, prayer, and sacrifice. Major gods are Indra (power), Varuna (the sky, order), Agni (fire, sacrifice), etc.

1000—600 B. C.

The **Rig-Veda** (Psalms)
The **Sama-Veda** (chants)
The **Yajur-Veda** (sacrificial hymns)
The **Atharva-Veda** ("homely" charms)

The great collections of hymns and charms.

Amos
Hosea

The **Brahmanas**

The **Mahabharata** Saga
Brihadaranyaka **Upanishad**
Taittiriya **Upanishad**

Elaboration of ritual and manuals for priest and sacrificer. Great importance placed on correctness of detail.

600—100 B. C.

Images Introduced into Hinduism
Chandogya **Upanishad**
Katha **Upanishad**
The **Ramayana** (Books II-VI)

Jeremiah

Svetasvatara **Upanishad**

The discovery of basic Hindu philosophic truth, discussion, and teaching in hermitages called Ashramas. The record of such teaching is the content of the **Upanishads.**

Early Buddhist History 500 B. C.

Sutra literature

The **Mahabharata** (major portion)

Buddhism a State Religion 300 B. C.

The Development of Saivism and Vaishnavism
The **Bhagavad-Gita** completed. Social system established according to fixed laws

Later Buddhist History

The Ramayana (books I and VII)

The systematized custom in all human relations — family, caste, household, political rules. The basis of Hindu law.

100 B. C.—500 A. D.

Syrian
Christian
Church in
Malabar

Creative
Period in
Buddhist and
Jain Literature

Mohammed

Parsis
Enter India

The Sankhya philosophy
The Code of Manu
The Yoga Sutra
The Puranas (old stories and legends)

The Vishnu Purana

500—1000 A. D.
The Mahabharata completed

Saivite Tamil Devotional Saints
Appar
Sambandhar
Sundaramurthi
Manikka—Vasagar

The six darshanas (accepted systems of philosophy differentiated and systematized.)

The development of popular literature based on characters in the Mahabharata and the Ramayana. Elaboration and expansion of legend.

Popularization of religious ideals through Puranas.

The
Crusades

Conquest
of northern
India
by
Muslim
Invaders

The Mogul
Empire

Early Roman
Catholic
Missions

Overseas
expansion of
Europe

1000—1700 A. D.
Bhakti Saints
Ramanuja (eminent Philosopher of the Bhakti Movement—Vaishnava)
Jnanesvara
(Marathi—Vaishnava)
Ramanand
(Hindi—Vaishnava)
Kabir (Hindi—Sought to unite Hindu Bhakti and Muslim Sufism.)
Chaitanya
(Bengali—Vaishnava)
Namdev
(Marathi—Vaishnava)
Sur Das
(Hindi—Vaishnava)
Tulsi Das
(Hindi—Vaishnava)
Tukaram
(Marathi—Vaishnava)
Dadudaya
(Marathi—Vaishnava)
Madhva (Bhakti philosopher)

Temples. Organization of worship.

Sectarian Hinduism (Vaishnava and Saivite) in popular forms of Bhakti. Devotion to a personal god in differing forms. Rival Bhakti schools in all sections of India.

Devotional poetry, song, and dance—movements centering around the Bhaktas.
Saiva Siddhanta, the philosophy of Saivism.

1700—1900 A. D.

British
Conquest
of Mahratta,
Mogul,
and Sikh
Empires

Hinduism stagnating.
  Rigidity in society.
  Defensiveness.

Beginning
of Protestant
Missions in
India:
Ziegenbalg
and
Plutschau,
1706

Hindu self-criticism

Schwartz,
1750

Carey, 1793

British
Sovereignty

**Movements of Reform and
   Defense**
The Brahmo Samaj
  Ram Mohan Roy
   Keshub Chandra Sen
   The Tagores
The Arya Samaj
  Dayananda Sarasvati
The Theosophical Society
Hindu Renaissance
  Sri Ramakrishna Para-
  mahamsa
  Swami Vivekananda

1900—1950 A. D.
**Later Hindu Renaissance
   and Nationalism**

Independence
and partition
1947

Mahatma Gandhi
Sri Ramana Maharshi
Sarvepalli Radhakrishnan

Assassination
of Gandhi
1948

Aurobindo Ghose
Vinoba Bhave

The Hindu Mahasabha

29

Parallel to the development of caste, as expressed vividly in the law codes, are the twin doctrines of transmigration and *karma* mentioned above as axiomatic. The division of society gives a very convenient theater in which the tragedy of life and its responsibilities are acted out. The Hindu finds reward or punishment for good or bad action in the hierarchy of life as expressed in the human realm in caste.

Dharma is in its legal context the performance of the duty assigned to caste; as one performs this duty well, one fits into the cosmic order and is in harmony with it. This lends the possibility of ultimate release from the responsibility of *karma*.

Hindu ethical principles and conduct patterns are brought to the people by stories. The great epics of the *Mahabharata* and the *Ramayana* are known, sung, and acted throughout the length and breadth of the land. Here are persons, intimate, knowable, who become the possession of the people, and through whose exploits and actions the culture of the past is communicated.

The *Mahabharata* is a "natural" epic. By this we mean that, like Topsy, it just grew. The nucleus of the story is the enmity between two sets of cousins representing more or less the forces of good and of evil. On the one side, the five sons of Pandu; and on the other side, the hundred brothers and a traitor or two who are skilled in court intrigue and trickery. It would perhaps not be profitable to outline this story-nucleus in this pamphlet, but it can be found very skillfully told elsewhere. (See the Reading List, page 60.)

The important thing about the *Mahabharata* is that it is peopled by real flesh and blood heroes, and, I may add, heroines, who have become a part of the living memory of the past and of Hindu tradition. Like the *Decameron* and the *Canterbury Tales*, this story-nucleus is a slender thread on which are woven many sub-stories that have been of great value in transmitting the *dharma* of Hindustan to her sons and daughters. The story of the chivalry in the court when Draupadi was insulted after having been gambled away into servitude by one of her five husbands, is a story containing drama and teaching enough for any expert in religious education.

The story of the princess Savitri, who chose as her husband the son of an exiled, impoverished, blind king, is one of the greatest teachings on wifely devotion extending even beyond death. When Satyavan died, Yama, the lord of death, came to take away his soul, wrapping it up in a bundle no bigger than a thumb. Savitri trudged after the soul through the valley of death, following Yama. In discussions with him on the way, she pleased him with her learning and her understanding, and he ultimately granted her several boons. She chose successfully to have the sight of her father-in-law restored and to have his kingdom returned to him. Ultimately she made a demand on Yama that did not violate his stipulation that she was not to request the return of the soul of Satyavan to his body; she asked that her sons might rule in this kingdom. The sons were not yet in existence. Yama acknowledged defeat, and this story has come to be an allegory of the relation of the faithfulness of the wife to the redemption of her husband. It is also, perhaps, an allegory of the ancient view of a good woman, whose flesh could not survive when her soul (her husband) had gone.

The *Puranas*, or old stories, are also the possession of the ordinary child of Hindustan. These are the legends centering around some of the major figures of Hindu legend (the *Prem-Sagar, Gita-Govinda,* etc.) who became the objects of devotion. Some of these stories, mostly centered around Krishna, often outrage Hindu as well as Christian views of social morality.

The stories of the early life of Krishna show him the object of the exaggerated, blind adoration of an especially susceptible set of child idolizers. His exploits are marvellous. The devotion given him by his mother, in spite of his misdeeds, is an archetype of religious devotion. As an adolescent, to state it mildly, he "played the field." The devotee of Krishna delights in the stories of his amorous adventures. One devotee will perhaps enjoy them as stories of what he himself would like to do; another, however, will allegorize

31

them and seek to emulate in his own life the complete self-giving to Krishna that was exemplified by Radha, the milk-maid.

In the early books there was also a great deal of philosophical material. Questions were asked about the nature and meaning of reality. These questions were usually left unanswered, although there is a suggestion that it is not enough to believe in the gods and their functions, but that Something lies beyond even the gods—Something unknowable, Something beyond the mind of man to conceive, to which he can give no name.

> This creation, whence it came into being, whether spontaneously or not—he who is its highest overseer in heaven, he surely knows, or perhaps he knows not.— *Rig-Veda* 10:129. (Translated by W. Norman Brown.)

These questions form the basis of the discussions in the forests. After a Brahman had studied with his teacher and had lived much of his life in society, "when he saw the sons of his sons," he was privileged to retire to think things out. He often left wife and children in care of the family and of the caste and sought out the lonely places and the pilgrim routes. Here, with others on like quest, he would evaluate his learning and his life. Certain great teachers arose, and informal "seminars," called *ashramas,* became the magnet for those who sought to "know." The record of such discussions is to be found in the *Upanishads.* These are not systems of philosophy—although they are the authoritative writings to which the philosopher invariably refers.

In spiritual succession to the *Upanishads* is the *Bhagavad-Gita.* It forms one section of the great epic of India, the *Mahabharata.* This is the most important single document in Hinduism. It represents a synthesis of all that has gone before. As such, its first reading may be confusing to a Western reader, but it is a monument to the Hindu genius for synthesis.

In the *Bhagavad-Gita* man is taught how to perform his duty, seek reality, and still live his life in the world. The central figure necessary to the poem is Arjuna, who represents man. He is involved in a great battle, and on the eve of battle raises questions concerning the righteousness of his fighting his own relatives. The answer to these questions constitutes complete instruction as to how and why Arjuna is to fight, accepting the fighting itself as necessary because it is Arjuna's caste duty.

Just two things need to be said concerning the teaching of the *Bhagavad-Gita*. The first is that one is not involved in responsibility for one's acts if he can perform them with no personal or individual involvement in the results of the action. He must be completely detached, with his mind fixed on the object of his devotion, in this instance Krishna. The second thing of major importance is that the dynamic for such action and such intense devotion is communicated with a vision of Krishna as he is in himself, a vision no human eye can tolerate.

The vision, or transfiguration, was granted by Krishna at Arjuna's insistence and after disciplinary preparation for the experience. The description is one of the most moving, most awe-full in the whole literature of devotion. The artist —whether his metier is sound, pigment, mass, building materials, or words—has been the most reliable communicator of Hindu ideas of the beyond the human to Hindus. Compare the eleventh chapter of the *Gita* with the Bible passage on the vision of Isaiah in the temple to grasp essential common problems of describing unusual religious insight and to gain new understanding of that which is unique in the Hindu and in the Hebrew concepts of God.

In the *Bhagavad-Gita* lies the essence of Hinduism—that the object of devotion to be sought lies completely beyond human experience and that any road selected to discipline oneself for the experience is valid. When one has reached the experience of Reality, he sees no difference in forms, the Brahman and the Sudra are the same, gold and a stone are the same, and all that exists is Krishna, and Krishna is Brahman. This insight is the *yoga* of knowledge, born of the *yoga* of right action and the *yoga* of devotion.

The unity of this document consists in the insistance that all the divergent elements expounded therein are caught up in Krishna. If one may paraphrase Paul, the purpose of the *Bhagavad-Gita* is to "sum up all things in Krishna."

From this book stems much of the very rich devotional literature of India. This devotional literature may have as its object any of the incarnations of Vishnu; Siva as the Absolute himself, with his consorts, his "powers"; or almost any person in mythology, in history, or even in the present. Some religious writers like Kabir and Nanak (founder of the Sikhs), have devoted their lives and talents to a personal theism forged from both Hindu and Muslim elements. This devotional richness is expressed, understandably enough, in the intimate spoken languages of the people and in the lives of those who have given up everything else but the love of God.

It will be impossible to do more than outline the subject matter of the lives and writings of the Hindu devotees.

It is very difficult for Western readers to understand that the concept of the impersonal as Absolute can exist alongside a devotional religion. To the Hindu, this presents no problem. It is recognized that for the ordinary individual the realization of the Absolute is impossible except in personal terms. This calls for the worship of the personal in whatever form an individual may choose as ultimately the manifestation of the Absolute. The forms chosen have been largely the incarnations of Vishnu, Rama and Krishna with their consorts, and the person of Siva with his consorts, Kali and Durga. The form of this worship varies with the aspect of these deities considered especially important to the individual. It makes little difference to the worshiper whether the object of his devotion is a historical figure or a mythological one. History is relatively non-important.

Bhakti means "loving devotion." It means faith and yet more than faith. It is, in its essence, an utter self-abandonment for love's sake. For the devotee, it becomes an all-consuming search, an intoxicating passion.

It is understandable that much of the *bhakti* literature is

34

Banaras. Here early morning worshipers, mostly pilgrims from many parts of India, are making their devotions at one of the bathing ghats that line the Ganges waterfront.

impassioned poetry, written, of course, in the language of the people. The headings under which one might group the writings of the *bhaktas* are: the recognition of the greatness and majesty of the object of devotion, with the corresponding littleness of the worshipers; the need for forgiveness and grace; the longing for the vision of God. The worshiper finds in the I-Thou relationship the real companionship of his life, which he spends in service to the deity. His ultimate end is serenity, rest, and peace.

This all-consuming search for the companionship of God requires that the mind be kept always and exclusively on God. The service involved is a service to God himself (often an image or symbol) and does not involve, necessarily, social service to one's fellowman as corollary. Sur Das found that his eyes were responsible for his thoughts wondering, so he removed his eyes the better to see God.

Some of the forms that Hindu devotional religion have taken are the *kirtan*, which is the singing of sacred songs with dance, the repetition of the divine Name, the worship of an image, the service of a slave, friendship, and self-surrender.

Each section of India has had its *bhakta* saints. There is not space here to characterize the *bhakti* of the various areas. But all are agreed with Tulsi Sahib, of Hathras:

> A lotus blooms in the water beneath; the sun and moon
> rise in the sky above; yet it opens at the touch
> of the sunshine or moonlight:
> So respond to His infinite love.
> As the spider time and again runs upward with the
> gossamer thread,
> Set thy face toward Him, O my heart!
> Leave other masters, serve only Him who is thine
> like a faithful bride.
> Thou canst see the Lord with the lamp of devotion
> alone, set on the salver of faith:
> And *bhakti* more than learning will dispel the darkness
> of thy doubt, O my heart![1]

[1] *Indian Witness*, Vol. LIX, No. 19, p. 291, translation by Cyril Modak, May 9, 1929.

It will be possible to summarize only briefly certain aspects of the *bhakti* movement.

Among the devotees of Siva there is very great emphasis on the sense of sin, the need for forgiveness, and the grace of the Lord. The legends concerning Siva and his appearance as the *guru* of the devotee, his help in time of need, some of the thought concerning his creative aspects through the dance as described in the first chapter, his drinking of the poison churned up at creation, which act saved mankind and turned his own throat blue—these are some of the things that constitute the subject matter of the poems in praise of Siva. These are for the most part in the Tamil language of South India and represent the basis for the philosophy of the Saiva Siddhanta as found in the South.

Certain of the devotees of Krishna have their devotion characterized by an allegorical reference to the erotic stories of the relationship to him of Radha, the chief of the milk-maids of Vrindaban, as symbolic of man's relation to God. The Chaitanya movement of Bengal is characterized by the same type of emotional excitement in the worship of Krishna that we sometimes associate with the ecstatic sects of the West. The songs of Mirabai, a princess who defied the Hindu Mrs. Grundy in order to follow the object of her devotion (thus incurring the enmity of her husband and her husband's family, if legend is to be believed), are much beloved and at the same time have a strong erotic flavor. The tenth book of the *Bhagavata-Purana*, known as the *Prem-Sagar*, is a record of the exploits of Krishna in his youth and adolescence that are looked upon as symbolic and allegorical.

The devotion of Krishna in the form of Vithoba in Western India has produced perhaps the most profoundly penetrating of all the schools of *bhakti*. Here the succession of Jnanesvara, who wrote a devotional commentary on the *Bhagavad-Gita*, Namdev, Eknath, and greatest of all, Tukaram, constitute a group of religious poets whose works still sing themselves into the hearts of the people who use Marathi, one of the major languages of Western India.

37

The Rama worshipers have an object of devotion who is ethically worthy to be followed for the highest Hindu good. The recension of the *Ramayana* done by Tulsi Das in Northern India created in this great epic poem a standard of the Hindi language that has not been surpassed. This poem has been briefly described in the opening chapter. Translations of Tulsi Das's work into other spoken languages of India make it equally available to all worshipers of Rama.

A last grouping of these devotional saints would include Kabir, the great singer of the Middle Ages, Nanak, the founder of the Sikhs, and their successors as those who have not been provincial or sectarian in their *bhakti*, but have believed that all names for God present a single diety whose characteristic is that he is the true Name, Sat Nam. These may be said to have begun the movement to look upon the differing religions as one, whose differences are local interpretations of the same experience of God.

Some *bhaktas* have realized that they would lose their most valued possession if they think in terms of identity of themselves with the object of devotion. Tukaram sings:

Can water quaff itself?
Can trees taste of the fruit they bear?
He who worships God must stand distinct from Him,
So only shall he know the joyful love of God;
For if he say that God and he are one,
That joy, that love, shall vanish instantly away.

Pray no more for utter oneness with God:
Where were the beauty if jewel and setting were one?
The heat and the shade are two,
If not, where were the comfort of shade?
Mother and child are two,
If not, where were love?
When, after long being sundered, they meet,
What joy do they feel, the mother and child!
Where were joy, if the two were one?
Pray, then, no more for utter oneness with God.[1]

[1] *An Indian Peasant Mystic;* Translation from Tukaram, by John S. Hoyland, pp. 19-20. London, Allenson and Co., Ltd., 1932. Used by permission.

It would be interesting to Western readers to know some of the Christians who have followed in the Indian devotional tradition and produced lyric works of great value, not only to the Christian communities of India but to Christendom as a whole. One such is Narayan Vaman Tilak of Western India (1862-1919) who has prayed thus for union with Christ;

As the moon and its beams are one,
     So, that I be one with Thee,
This is my prayer to Thee, my Lord,
     This is this beggar's plea.

I would snare Thee and hold Thee ever,
     In loving wifely ways;
I give Thee a daughter's welcome,
     I give Thee a sister's praise.

As words and their meaning are linked,
     Serving one purpose each,
Be Thou and I so knit, O Lord,
     And through me breathe Thy speech.

O be my soul a mirror clear,
     That I may see Thee there;
Dwell in my thought, my speech, my life,
     Making them glad and fair.

Take Thou this body, O my Christ,
     Dwell as its soul within;
To be an instant separate,
     I count a deadly sin.[1]

Bhakti is one of the disciplines that in the Hindu patterns leads to the cessation of birth and death and release into eternal reality. Those who have followed it to an experience of God are themselves looked to as worthy of devotion.

It may be said in conclusion that the *bhakti* movement had a tremendous effect on the social life of the people in that the fellowship of devotion in groups created by the

---

[1] *Narayan Vaman Tilak*, by J. C. Winslow, p. 106. Calcutta, India, Association Press, 1923. Used by permission.

movement was such that all thought of caste disappeared. The Bengali Vaishnavas even went so far as to say that the worshiper of Krishna is himself a worshiper of Brahman in the form of Krishna and therefore is the true Brahman. He may be given the sacred thread of the highest caste, irrespective of the social grouping into which he was born. Among the devotional saints themselves one finds a wide spread of social differences, from the Brahman to the outcaste.

In closing this chapter, it is necessary to mention briefly a few characteristics of everyday life and practice in Hinduism that cannot be omitted even in this introductory sketch.

Individual worship. The religion of the Hindu is intensely individual. In spite of the fact that much of the action of a Hindu is determined by his caste duty, this control largely is social and economic. The individual seeks his own salvation, and works out his own *karma*. There is no such thing as congregational or group worship in the conventional Hindu pattern. One performs his *puja* (worship sacrifice) alone; he goes alone to the heart of the temple, which is a small room without outside light, dramatizing the fact that the worship of Hinduism is ultimately inner. There is room at the shrine for very few people at one time.

Pilgrimage. The Hindu believes also in seeking out places of significance and people of significance. Much of this rests on the legends or history of his *ishta devata,* his particular object of devotion. Worshipers of Krishna go to Vrindaban in North India and other places where the stories of Krishna are centered or where one of his *bhaktas* has taught. Worshipers of Siva seek out Chidambaram, Tanjore, Banaras, and other spots. Rama worshipers go to places associated with the story of their hero. Many are interested in following the Ganges to its source, in making pilgrimages to remote spots in the Himalayas where natural glacier formations suggest the residence of Siva.

And always there are the great teachers whose *ashramas* can be visited for refreshment and learning. The benefit to be derived from being in the presence of one who is more experienced in the religious life are summed up in the idea of the *darsana*, or vision of Reality in personal form.

Ahimsa. This is at the top of the list of ethical precepts in Hinduism, Buddhism, and Jainism. In its simplicity, it is the vow of non-injury to life, non-killing. It is the foundation of vegetarianism, carried to an extreme among the Jains. Its results are well publicized in the West as having direct bearing on economy, health, and food supply. Gandhi called *ahimsa* the highest truth, the basis of his method of non-violent resistance to evil. In this sense, it means non-injury in thought, word, or deed—the defense of truth without injury to an opponent.

The Cow. Veneration of the cow has been enjoined on Hindus from the time of their ancient codes of law. It is still practiced. It is, of course, an integral part of the practice of *ahimsa*, but goes much further than that—sometimes even valuing the life of the cow beyond that of any person but a Brahman. Some interesting attempts are being made to house cows in special spots, with adequate care and control of reproduction in order to reduce India's bovine population, the largest in the world. This could, perhaps, be done without too great a strain on orthodox prejudice. Gandhi's attitude is puzzling:

> The central fact of Hinduism is cow protection. Cow protection to me is one of the most wonderful phenomena in human evolution. It takes the human being beyond his species. The cow to me means the entire sub-human world. Man through the cow is enjoined to realize his identity with all that lives. Why the cow was selected for apotheosis is obvious to me. The cow was in India the best companion. She was the giver of plenty. Not only did she give milk, but she also made agriculture possible. The cow is a poem of pity. One reads pity in the gentle animal. She is the mother to millions of Indian mankind. Protection of the cow means protection of the whole dumb creation of God. . . .
>
> Hindus will be judged not by their *tilaks*, not by the

41

correct chanting of *mantras,* not by their pilgrimages, not by their most punctilious observance of caste rules, but by their ability to protect the cow.[1]

One finds in the Indian bazaars pictures of Kamadugha, the Cow who grants desires. In residence in the various parts of her anatomy are the gods of Hinduism. The udder is the *Upanishads,* Krishna is the one who milks, and Arjuna is the calf. One such picture shows the milk being sought by Parsis, by Muslims, and by Christians.

Discipline, Renunciation, and Asceticism. It has already been pointed out that the effort of the individual toward his own salvation must be in complete discipline of himself as a prerequisite to any kind of understanding of Reality or preparation for an intuitive experience. Man must find his own essence within himself, without aid, except that of his own making. The concept of *tapas,* literally meaning fire or heat, is that the fire or heat of discipline cleanses the ego from all interest in the lower aspects of the self and the individual.

We have seen in all great Hindus of the past and of the present this willingness to renounce every kind of self-centered motivation in order to achieve the greater realization of the true Self. Man reaches God by his own effort.

Even in some *bhakti* groups, where the idea of grace is by no means absent, the grace that one receives from the object of devotion is that which is a reflection of the degree of devotional discipline that has been attained by the worshiper. It is an answer to devotion, rather than a grace that has its origin in the initiative of God. The intensity and the depth of India's search for Reality can be seen in the absoluteness of discipline on the part of Hindu seekers.

There is little or no justification within Hinduism, its sacred books or its teachings, for the types of asceticism that is often thought to be characteristic of Hinduism. The type of self-punishment represented by hook swinging and lying

---

[1] *Hindu Dharma,* by M. K. Gandhi, pp. 297-98. Ahmedabad, India, Navajivan Publishing House, 1950. Used by permission.

on beds of spikes is commonly believed to be an approach to the attainment of spiritual qualities often practiced by the Hindu Indian. To the writer of this pamphlet, this represents a misreading of the conflict between flesh and spirit as seen in the Hindu scriptures and Hindu teaching. The practices do exist, but in decreasing ratio to the new understandings of the requirements of self-discipline.

The psychological renunciation of the Buddha, the renunciation of the lower desires of man, is being interpreted today in terms of the twentieth century. No longer does it mean the same type of withdrawal from the world it once did. Renunciation will still play an important part in the life of Hindu India as long as her essential philosophy endures.

Monkmeyer

A partial view of the Minakshi-Sundareswara Temple at Madurai, South India, constructed mainly in the sixteenth and seventeenth centuries and dedicated to Siva and his consort

IV. Hindu Renaissance

During the first half of the nineteenth century Hinduism was in a state of stagnation. No critics are more vitriolic in description of this stagnation than those Hindus who themselves participated in the re-awakening of Hinduism. Such descriptions from Western sources were not equally welcome. New ideas were spreading over India, the West was making political and cultural inroads on the very soil of India itself, and the possibility of travel and study abroad was opened to Indians. Through that century Christianity was making its second major appearance on Indian soil.

There were several reactions to the results of contact with the West: one was a retreat into orthodoxy and the things of the past; another was a wholehearted, full acceptance of things Western. During the course of the years, both of these patterns have been followed, but with indifferent success.

A third reaction was one of social reform and reconstruction from within. At the beginning this stimulated the formation of separatist movements in the form of organizations that sought to bring about change by themselves taking the courageous path of rebellion. Among these movements were the Brahmo Samaj, founded in Bengal, usually associated with the names of Ram Mohan Roy, Keshub Chandra Sen, and the Tagore family. This was a unitarian movement,

44

Terrace of the main portion of the new Lakshminarain
Temple in New Delhi, popularly called by the name of its
donor, the Birla Temple

using the *Upanishads* and the New Testament as basic sources and applying a fresh outlook to society, without discrimination because of caste or sex. There were counterparts of the Brahmo Samaj in various other parts of India.

The Arya Samaj was and is a more orthodox movement than that of the Brahmo Samaj and has as its slogan, "back to the *Vedas*." In the fiery days of India's nationalism, the Arya Samaj enunciated the principle that to be an Indian is to be a Hindu. This resulted in a program for the reconversion of Muslims and Christians to Hinduism, a program still sponsored by the Samaj.

The most important personality, however, was that of Sri Ramakrishna Paramahamsa. He has become the justification of Hinduism to the modern movement. At a time when Western scholars were beginning to discover the treasures of Hindu literature, building up in the Indian a new respect for his own heritage, Ramakrishna breaks into the scene in justification of the major emphases of Hinduism.

His was a universal religion, which included all the historical religions of the world. In his most amazing experiences of *samadhi*, ecstasy, he claimed to have caught a vision of Reality, through his Mother, the goddess Kali, through the metaphysical experience of the realization of the Absolute, through the identification of himself with the characters in the old Hindu stories, and through what he interpreted as Islam and Christianity. There was a picture painted to show this universalism, which had in the background the houses of worship of Hinduism, Islam, and Christianity, before which buildings were representatives of the various faiths found in India, and in the foreground Jesus in a devotional dance with Chaitanya, the Vaishnava leader of Bengal. In all of his life and teaching, Ramakrishna was the essence of Hinduism, and much of his life was spent in the vicinity of his favorite representation of reality, the image of the goddess Kali.

From the life and teachings of Ramakrishna have arisen a movement known as the Ramakrishna Mission, or the Vedanta Society, which has reached out into the West and has centers in the United States. The Saint Paul of the movement was Swami Vivekananda (1863-1902) who systematized the teachings of the Vedanta in terms of modern life and thought, established centers of social service in India, and traveled in Europe and America expounding his views.

This justification of Hinduism in the modern day has been strengthened and undergirded by the work of Sri Aurobindo Ghose, Sri Ramana Maharshi, Sir Sarvepalli Radhakrishnan, Rabindranath Tagore, Mahatma Gandhi, and others—philosophers, poets, *yogis*.

It will be impossible to do more than characterize in a few words these men and their work. Sri Ramana is in the more conservative tradition of the non-dualist who has found the highest truth. Writing of him, his followers capitalize the personal pronoun.

Sri Aurobindo, after a stormy political career, retired to Pondicherry in what was then French India and established an *ashrama* of many disciples. Here he remained in seclusion, showing himself once or twice a year, and writing a formidable array of essays, plays, poems, and theological works. He was intensely aware of the crisis in human affairs and believed a creative synthesis of the spirit of India with the technology of the West and the insights of the theistic religions is possible. His theory centered around a dynamic integration of the conscious contemporary life with the attainment of full spiritual freedom in the true Hindu tradition.

Dr. Radhakrishnan is teacher, educational administrator, philosopher, and writer. In 1949 he was appointed as the first Indian ambassador to Russia and later became vice-president of the Republic of India. His exposition of Hinduism is probably the most influential today, both in India and abroad. His is also a new synthesis based on the spiritual needs of the contemporary world, a universalism based on the Vedanta, which he believes to be the foundation of all the religions of the world. His followers are scattered among the departments of philosophy in the universities of India.

Characteristic of present-day interpretations of Hinduism are the following:

1. A recognition of the difference between the static and the dynamic aspects of Hinduism. There is either a complete divorce between those elements that have incrusted Hindu society like barnacles for centuries and the vital religious elements, or a reinterpretation and reformation of the former in an effort to clear away that which outrages the moral sense.

2. A fresh attempt to find an adequate place for the possibility of an optimistic view of the world. The end of Hinduism in the past has been termed, perhaps wrongly, supra-ethical—the nature of the Real by definition (or lack of definition) having little or no ultimate relation to the good life.

3. The separation of "church" and state. Many liberal Hindus reject political Hinduism, by which term we mean the attempt of orthodoxy (politically, the Hindu Mahasabha and allied parties) to create a Hindu state, maintaining the old Hindu codes intact, with little modification of traditional marriage and caste regulations, cow-protection, and the rest. Hindus of this school envisage, rather, a prophetic mission of universal religion within a secular state tolerant of everything except conversion from one religion to another. This, they maintain, is unnecessary under any circumstances.

An area of great tension in modern Hinduism lies in the question as to whether or not a developing and evolving Hinduism can incorporate an ethic essential to it and at the same time essential to the world in which we live. The traditional divorce between the religious experience of the Hindu as one of spiritual realization and the morality of a relatively unreal world has become intolerable.

Whether the new concepts of responsibility—political, social, economic—can receive dynamic from religion and religious experience remains to be seen. Yet, ethical values and social values are not integral to the ultimate Hindu view of life. This is certainly one of the major questions of modern life in India, and its solution must mean either a redefinition of the nature of Reality itself or an artificial and extra-religious grounding of ethics in a sort of universal humanism.

Perhaps the greatest examplar of the religious principles of Hinduism in contemporary India is Vinoba Bhave, who has captured the imagination of India with his genius for symbolic action and his complete selflessness. It is he who, at an advanced age, has been tramping barefoot the dusty roads of village India, challenging those who have property to a more equitable voluntary division of the land. But he has continued to link his intense social action with his religious principles, following the patterns of devotional religious practice of his predecessor, Mahatma Gandhi. Both these men, through the selfless power of the renunciation of force, of personal power, of anger, and of greed, have accomplished the unbelievable.

V. The Christian Church in its
Hindu Setting

We may now properly return
to the perspective that alone can justify the writing of this
pamphlet. The Christian in India is concerned that the witness to his faith be pure, of unmixed motive, understanding,
and unambiguous. He is under the most severe obligation to
be honest and to be Christlike in his reading of the implica-
tion of his witness. In an effort to discharge that obligation
sincerely, he is not concerned to "make Christians" out of
Hindus in the nominal sense. He must, however, be intensely
aware of the human situation and proclaim the word of God
to man in India as elsewhere.

The major task of the Christian church is the communication of this gospel to man. This is a world task of a world
church. Long since have we passed the point where there
are certain privileged nations and cultures that are thought
to have embodied the Christian message in a peculiar fash-
ion, from whom alone this flow of communication takes
place. In response to the necessity of communication, the
word of God was proclaimed in India and among Hindus.
This had two major results: one result has been an inevitable diffusion of Christian ideas and ideals throughout
the country and its people, so that in reaction and in modification many new concepts have made themselves felt

Henri R. Ferger

Gateway and chapel of the Christu-kula Ashram (The Family of Christ) at Tirupatur, South India

within the older religions themselves; the other result has been the creation of a body of those who have given their total loyalty to Jesus Christ and his way of life.

This body, the Christian church in India, is mature and has assumed for itself the task of the proclamation of the Christian gospel within the borders of India to her people. The outreach of the church has gone even beyond the borders of India to other areas and other peoples. In common with the church of Christ in the world, the Indian church sees the need of the gospel as a need of mankind. It is only incidental that many of those who hear this proclamation in India are Hindus. It is to Hindus as they share the common predicament of man that this gospel is most realistically preached.

The history of the last century has made some of the most commonly held ideas concerning Hinduism anachronisms. No longer can the Christian gospel claim an exclusive right to speak against the social ills of the Hindu or to sponsor fundamental human rights. Many aspects of the Constitution of the Republic of India would have been unpredictable a generation ago and seem to contradict some of the aspects of Hinduism that we have been accustomed to regard as essential to Hindu culture. We have discovered that sanctions can be found within the traditions of Hinduism for many of these modern changes. In fact, the changes can perhaps only take place in areas where some kind of Hindu sanction can be found. This is one reason why some of what seem to be the traditional aspects of Hindu social history have been omitted from this little treatise. One can scarcely lay stress, for instance, upon the disabilities of women when one sees the place that they occupy in modern Hindu life. The reforms in the Hindu marriage laws enacted and proposed in the legislative bodies of India make no observation universally valid concerning some of these traditions.

There are certain factors that mold the vocabulary of the proclamation in life and word among Hindus today.

The social, economic, educational, and medical needs of

the Hindu people bring a response, in the name of Christ, to join with the efforts of the Hindu in government and philanthropic agencies. To what degree these disabilities are directly due to Hinduism is open to question—they may more properly be laid at the door of history and human fraility. We are more concerned here with the implications for a true Christian evangelism expressed more directly in relevance to Hindu patterns of life and thought. Some factors are the following:

The Hindu view of Christ. Jesus is reverenced as a religious adept who has realized Reality and has authority to teach his way of life, which is one of purity and moral grandeur. Tributes to him are ungrudging, and the epithet "Christlike" is reserved for saints. He is placed alongside the heroes of Hindu spiritual history, mythological and historical figures. Those more mindful of history think of the succession of personalities who have spoken to their generations at times of need without benefit of religious label— Buddha, Jesus, Mohammed, Gandhi. The Hindu would not have us think less of the Christ, but more of many others.

Involved in the above is the Hindu view of history. History is the theater of the evolution of the soul, the relatively real, concealing the Real from mortal eye. It proceeds to its inevitable destruction. Man's duty is to rise above the flux of historical change and enjoy the silent stillness of the Eternal Brahman.

The Christian in India as elsewhere sees history as the necessary scene of the enactment of the communication of God to man. This he believes is uniquely accomplished in the person of Jesus Christ. He alone gives definition to God. He is the way to the release of man from the predicament in which he finds himself into a knowledge of God. The communication of this good news is in the very nature of God himself and in his essential character as goodness, holiness, and love.

The Hindu view of history I have sometimes irreverently termed the bubble-gum theory, wherein the world is created in cycles that appear for a time and ultimately disappear by reabsorption into Brahman. The Christian view is essentially linear with something happening at a point in history that has made clear the purpose of God to man. This would seem to be essential to the Christian view and, therefore, the Hindu view of history is inadequate to carry this Christian gospel.

As has already been intimated, this presents to the modern Hindu one of the greatest tensions of his thinking concerning man and his destiny and concerning a proper evaluation of the world. He knows that there must be an ethical grounding of Reality, and his resolution of this tension will determine how closely he approximates a Christian world view.

Truth as the Christian seeks and sees it is dependent on the recognition of the necessity of decision in the immediate present, the eternal "now." This decision is based on a Christian understanding of history in which the central fact is Christ himself. Evil and suffering are not minimized, explained, or read out of existence. They are facts, accepted in all their tragedy, not to be escaped through ritual, sacrament, or exaggerated mysticism. We are not, however, left grimly holding on in the midst of historic necessity, but trusting confidently in the power and purpose of God as revealed in Jesus Christ.

The relation of the Christian church to India's cultural history is of great concern. Professor Radhakrishnan, in a government report outlining the program of religious education in India's educational plans, writes, "The chief source of spiritual nourishment for any people must be its own past perpetually rediscovered and renewed."

The church does indeed want to find itself in the stream of India's history. But one Christian group discussing the problem gave this as its answer:

> The gospel in relation to any national culture both adopts native forms and means for effective expression, and creates new ones consistent with its own nature . . . a distinction has to be made between customs and ways of religious and social life, and

the truth which has always been the source of Christian vitality in relation to any culture.[1]

The attempt to discover the "naked" gospel, free of non-Indian cultural barnacles, and to proclaim it through an autonomous church in dress congenial to the genius of India, will allow the Christian message to be understood by non-Christian India. The understanding that has met such Christian expressions in living as those of Sadhu Sundar Singh, Narayan Vaman Tilak, A. C. Chakraverti, and C. F. Andrews bears ample testimony to the validity of their witness.

In 1879 Keshub Chandra Sen said in a lecture:

> It seems that the Christ that has come to us is an Englishman, with English manners and customs about him and with the temper and spirit of an Englishman in him. Hence is it that the Hindu people shrink back and say, "Who is this revolutionary reformer who is trying to sap the very foundations of native society and bring about an outlandish faith and civilization quite incompatible with Oriental instinct and ideas?"[2]

Keshub himself actually saw the relevance of the Christian gospel to Hindu society, but he never became a Christian. Those Christians mentioned above have also wrestled with the problem of the relation of their Hindu background to their new birth in Christ.

In answer to a question as to whether or not he felt himself ready to be baptized as a Christian, A. C. Chakraverti, a Hindu devotee of profound sincerity, replied, "Yes, I am ready, provided you do not touch my style of dress, my name, ways of food, etc. Just as I am now, you can baptize me. If your rules and customs permit, I am ready to be baptized."[3] He meant by this that his name was not to be

---

1 "Presenting the Gospel," in the *National Christian Council Review* (India), January, 1951.

2 *The Oriental Christ*, by P. C. Mozoomdar, p. 23. Boston, George H. Ellis Co., 1883.

3 *How I Found God and How God Found Me,* by A. C. Chakraverti, p. 193. Published by the author, Ramanreti, Vrindaban, U. P. India, Revised Edition, 1952.

changed into a Western name nor was he to be anglicized. Upon assurance that none of these things would be required as essentially Christian, Mr. Chakraverti became one of the most spirited leaders in Christian evangelism among the people whose agelong search for God he had shared until his final "birthday" when he met the Christ.

There are many others who are now writing the Epistle to the Hindus. They follow logically and loyally in the pioneer footprints of such a stalwart as Sadhu Sundar Singh. His adoption of the saffron robe of the *sannyasi* of Hinduism means that this Christianity of his is no alien to his native land. It is the essential spontaneity of his Christian expression in both the thought forms and the religious life of India that makes of him one of the great prophets and saints of Christian history.

Another trailblazer was B. C. Sircar, who in his *ashrama* at Puri practiced disciplinary measures after the manner of *yoga* that were always distinctly Christian. A. C. Chakraverti has established his center of Christian radiation at Vrindaban, the place to which he himself came seeking some final refuge in God as a preacher of the Chaitanya movement. Having found the end of his search in this center of Hindu pilgrimage, he gives of his life and of his Christian discipline to those who beat their way to his door.

Others have used the means of communication found most largely in the *bhakti* movement of Hinduism to proclaim their devotion to the Christ. Among these the most conspicuous place goes to Narayan Vaman Tilak, a Brahman of the Marathi country in Western India, who said that he came to Christ over the bridge of Tukaram and who is rated as one of the major Marathi poets of a rich literary history. And there is H. A. Krishna Pillai, who is responsible for many of the lyrics in Tamil hymnology. Others have used the *kirtan*, the singing sermon, the *kalakshepam* in South India, to sing the glories of the Christ into the hearts of the Indian people in the traditional ways of the country. I remember being at one interesting *kirtan* where the story of Zaccheus was being sung and acted. The whole audience

56

Sadhu Sundar Singh

finally participated in the drama as half of them climbed trees and the other half joined the procession beneath them.

Christian *ashramas* and other institutions and expressions of the religious life in Hindu forms have spoken to the heart of India.

In the canon of the New Testament there is no Epistle to the Hindus to crystallize the relation between Hinduism and Christianity. Theologians in the extreme wing of the dialectic school see an absolute break between the word of God and the religions of the world, Hinduism included. At the other extreme, committed Christians see God's hand in the rare preparation of the Hindu people to recognize truth, to see the reality of the unseen, to give their all in devotion thereto. Some would use all this as an Old Testament to the New Life in Christ. In between lie varying shades of opinion. It is abundantly evident that the lives of such contemporary figures as Gandhi and Vinoba constitute a challenge demanding witness in life and work to the dynamic of the searching God and the indwelling Christ.

A new awareness of the message of Christianity to India came with the assassination of Mahatma Gandhi. Through that life given in martyrdom for his people, a fresh sense of the meaning of the cross of Christ was evident. It may be that in this new sense of meaning that came to India in so cataclysmic a manner, some purpose of God for his good news in India was being worked out.

In these tragic days of the mid-twentieth century, the Christian can approach the Hindu with no sense of superiority. He is too deeply aware of the tragedy of our time and the common predicament in which we are all caught. It is in the sense of discovery of God's plan for man in meeting the tragedy of life that we are brought together to share our resources. It is here that the Christian with confidence proclaims the gospel.

Christianity and Hinduism face many common problems today. One among them that is perhaps uppermost in the minds of those in the West is the menace to us all of communism. The issues of communism vitally affect all religious communities. If together we took stock of the resources of both Christianity and Hinduism to meet this particular challenge, we would find ourselves confronted with the fundamental concepts of each of these two religions. Our common need to meet the issues raised would necessitate a searching of the very springs of reality, the interpretation of history in its cosmic significance along with an adequate definition of ethics.

Hinduism has throughout the centuries of its meeting with Christianity been baffled by its inability to absorb the body of the Christian church. On the other hand, Christianity has met the resistance of a well-established social order and the paralyzing effect of the Hindu Vedanta with its all-encompassing hospitality. Those who would accept an exclusive loyalty to Jesus Christ have been comparatively few. The result has often been an alienation and a suspicion, one community of the other.

When we face common failures and reproaches in meeting the issues of communism, the possibility of a Christian witness is exciting and real, as indeed it is in meeting all the issues of life. The Christian evangelist in these circumstances cannot be regarded as arrogant, for he is seeking with humility and honesty an opportunity to demonstrate the depth of his faith. Our rivalries in the realm of ideas and ways of life become opportunities for sharing the resources of Christianity to meet the needs of the moment. We all bring to it a shared tragedy of human experience.

A full volume, to say nothing of such a brief pamphlet as this, would be inadequate to depict the excitement and fluidity to be found within Hinduism at this moment. Hinduism's charter for untrammeled and uninhibited change is written large in her source of ultimate authority. Definition of the nature and character of God owes much already to her apprehension of Christ. Is it too much to believe that with the dynamic of the abandon of commitment to God so characteristic of India, her new ways will find in him the satisfaction of her ageless aspirations?

Reading List

The author has listed here for further reading a few popular and inexpensive titles. Those who wish to go more deeply into the subject will find comprehensive and scholarly books on the Hindu religion in public libraries.

Adventures of Rama, The, by Joseph Gaer. Boston, Little, Brown and Co., 1954. $3.00.

Discovery of India, The, by Jawaharlal Nehru. New York, The John Day Co., 1946. $5.00.

Eastern Religions and Western Thought, by Sarvepalli Radhakrishnan. New York, Oxford University Press, 1940. $2.40.

Five Brothers, The, the story of the Mahabharata, by Elizabeth Seeger. New York, The John Day Co., 1948. $4.00.

Hindu Scriptures, edited by Nicol MacNicol. London, New York, E. P. Dutton and Co., 1938. $1.65.

Hinduism, by A. C. Bouquet. New York, Longmans Green and Co., 1950. Text edition, $1.80.

India: A Short Cultural History, by H. G. Rawlinson. New York, D. Appleton-Century Co., Inc., 1938. (Available through libraries.)

Myths and Symbols in Indian Art and Civilization, by Heinrich Zimmer. New York, Pantheon Books, Inc., 1946. $4.50.

Ramacaritamanasa, by Goswami Tulasi Das; translated by W. D. P. Hill. New York, Oxford University Press, 1952. $3.95.

Ramayana and the Mahabharata, The, translated by Romesh Chunder Dutt. New York, E. P. Dutton and Co., 1900. $1.65.

Religion of the Hindus, The, symposium edited by Kenneth W. Morgan. New York, The Ronald Press Co., 1953. $5.00.

Song of God: Bhagavad-Gita, translated by Swami Prabhavananda and Christopher Isherwood, with an introduction by Aldous Huxley. New York, The New American Library, 1954. 35 cents.

Hindu Music

Religious and Classical Music of India. Twelve-inch, 33⅓ rpm playing record. With notes by Alain Danielou. Ethnic Folkways Library, 117 W. 46th St., New York 36, N. Y. $5.95.